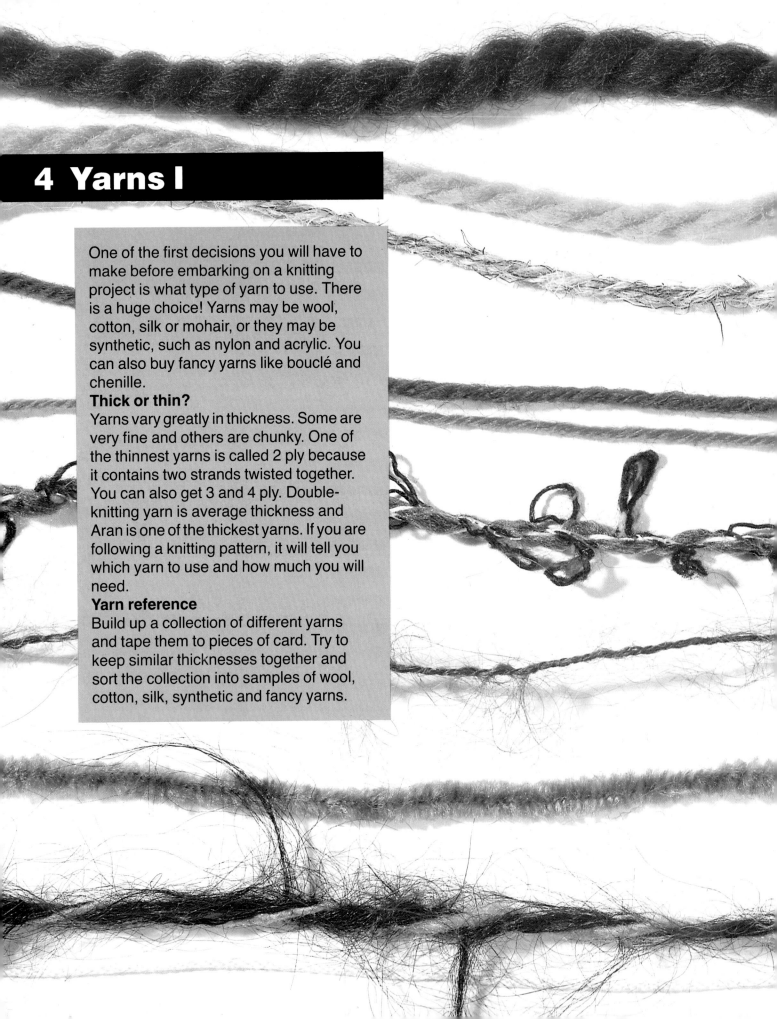

# 4 Yarns I

One of the first decisions you will have to make before embarking on a knitting project is what type of yarn to use. There is a huge choice! Yarns may be wool, cotton, silk or mohair, or they may be synthetic, such as nylon and acrylic. You can also buy fancy yarns like bouclé and chenille.

## Thick or thin?

Yarns vary greatly in thickness. Some are very fine and others are chunky. One of the thinnest yarns is called 2 ply because it contains two strands twisted together. You can also get 3 and 4 ply. Double-knitting yarn is average thickness and Aran is one of the thickest yarns. If you are following a knitting pattern, it will tell you which yarn to use and how much you will need.

## Yarn reference

Build up a collection of different yarns and tape them to pieces of card. Try to keep similar thicknesses together and sort the collection into samples of wool, cotton, silk, synthetic and fancy yarns.

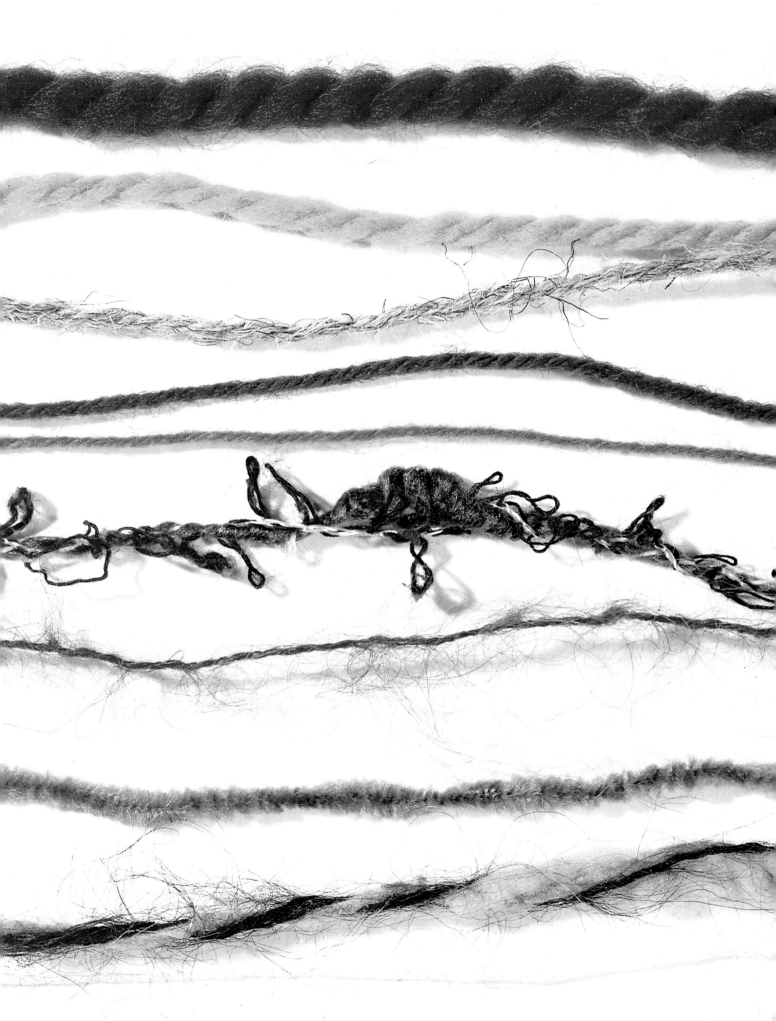

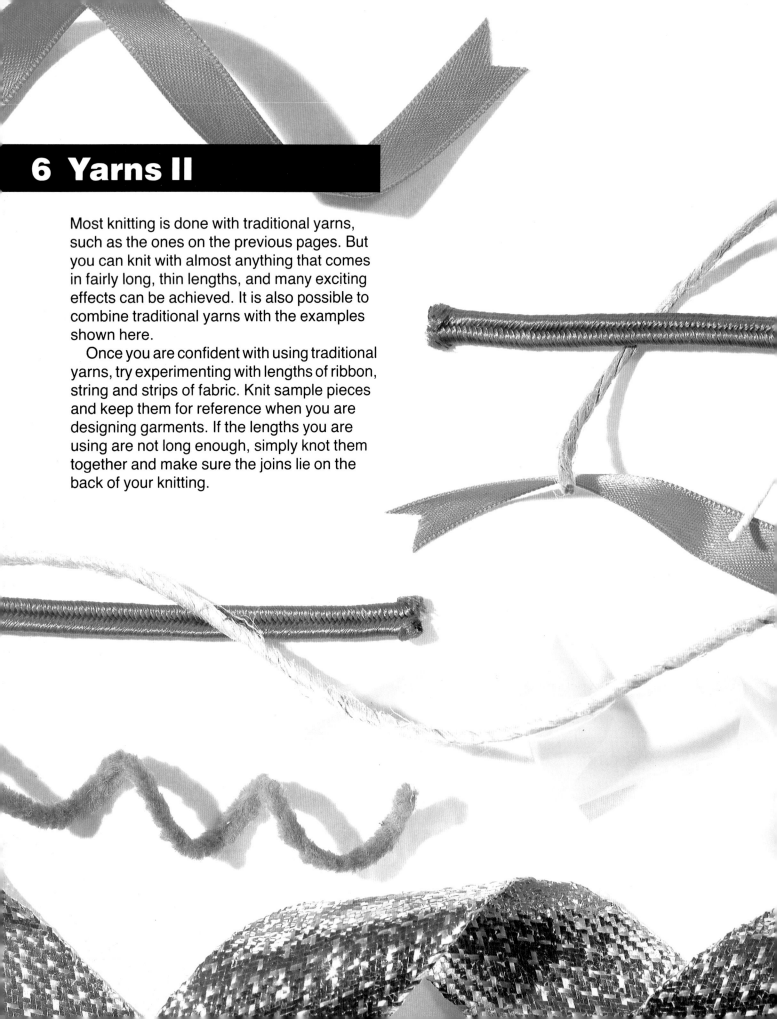

# 6 Yarns II

Most knitting is done with traditional yarns, such as the ones on the previous pages. But you can knit with almost anything that comes in fairly long, thin lengths, and many exciting effects can be achieved. It is also possible to combine traditional yarns with the examples shown here.

Once you are confident with using traditional yarns, try experimenting with lengths of ribbon, string and strips of fabric. Knit sample pieces and keep them for reference when you are designing garments. If the lengths you are using are not long enough, simply knot them together and make sure the joins lie on the back of your knitting.

# 8 Needles

Once you have decided what type of yarn to use, you will have to select your knitting needles. As with yarns, there is a huge choice of needles. They are sold in different thicknesses ranging from very fine to very thick. The sizes are printed on a knob at the end of the needle.

Generally, it is best to use fine needles with thin yarn and fat needles with chunky yarn – the samples here will give you an idea of the effect you will get. If you are following a pattern, it will tell you what size needles to buy.

Knitting needles are made from wood, plastic or metal and it is up to you to choose which suits you best. They are also sold in different lengths. If you are knitting a garment with lots of stitches you should choose long needles and for a narrow strip, short needles.

## Special needles

You can buy needles which are pointed at both ends. These are used for making cables. A crochet hook is useful for looping tassels through. You may also need a stitch holder which is used to store stitches if you do not want to cast them off. For sewing up your knitting, you will need a large darning needle with a big eye.

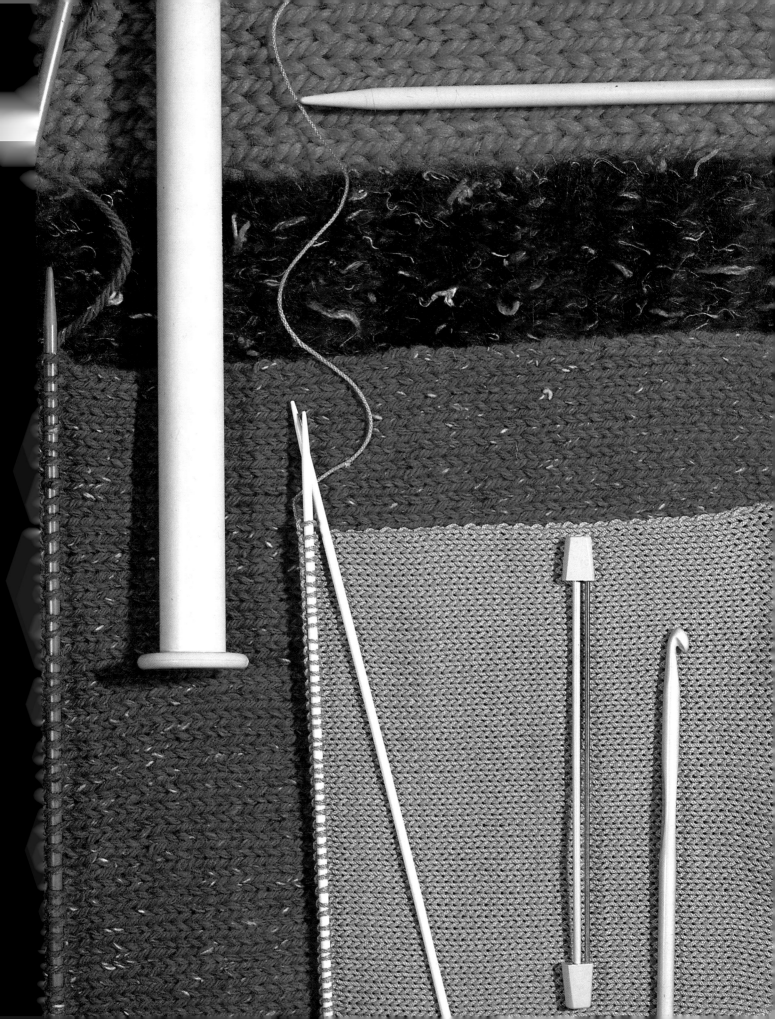

Casting on means making the first row of stitches. Make a slip knot on the left hand needle. Put the right hand needle through the slip knot. Wind the yarn around the back and between the needles.

Keeping the yarn taut with your right hand, use the point of the right hand needle to pick up the loop that has been made. Pull this loop through in front of the left hand needle.

Take the right hand needle – holding the stitch you have just made – to the back of the left hand needle. Using the point of the left hand needle, gently pull the stitch off the right hand needle.

Continue making stitches in this way until you have the correct number of stitches on the left hand needle. If you are following a pattern, it will tell you how many stitches to cast on.

When you have finished a piece of knitting, you will have to take the stitches off the needle, making sure they are secure and will not unravel. This is called casting off.

**5**

The cast-off edge should not be too tight. If it is too tight, use a larger needle. Casting off is done by working on two stitches at a time. Start by knitting two stitches on to the right hand needle.

**6**

Keeping the yarn at the back, use the point of the left hand needle to pick up the first stitch you knitted. Start pulling this gently over the second stitch on the right hand needle.

**7**

Pull the stitch over and let if fall between the needles. Knit another stitch and slip the stitch on the needle over it as before. At the end of the row, pass the yarn through the last stitch.

**8**

# 12 Plain & Purl I

**1**

Plain stitch is easy. Push the point of the right hand needle up through the first stitch on the other needle.

**2**

Wind the yarn round the back of the right hand needle and in between the two needles.

**3**

Keeping the yarn taut with your right hand, bring the right hand needle down and through the loop that has formed.

**4**

When you have got the loop firmly on the right hand needle, slip the original stitch off the left hand needle.

**1**

Purl stitch is similar to plain. Push the needle down through the front of the stitch, keeping the wool at the front.

**2**

Wind the yarn, from front to back, round the right hand needle and keep it taut with your right hand.

**3**

In the same way as before, pull through the loop that has formed between the two needles.

**4**

Pull off the stitch on the left hand needle. Look at the next page to see how to combine plain with purl!

# 14 Plain & Purl II

The sample at the top of the page shows rows of plain knitting. This is sometimes called *garter* stitch.

The small sample in the middle shows the effect you get if you alternate rows of plain stitches with rows of purl stitches. This is known as *stocking stitch*. The smooth side is normally used as the right side. Stocking stitch is often used for making garments such as sweaters and cardigans.

The sample on the far right shows the reverse side of stocking stitch. It looks similar to plain knitting but the ridges are closer together.

The sample at the bottom of the page shows a stitch called *rib*. It is made by alternating plain and purl stitches on the first row. Make sure you have an even number of stitches and always start the row with a plain stitch. Ribbing gives a stretchy finish and is often used as a border. Basic rib can be varied by knitting two plain stitches followed by two purl stitches.

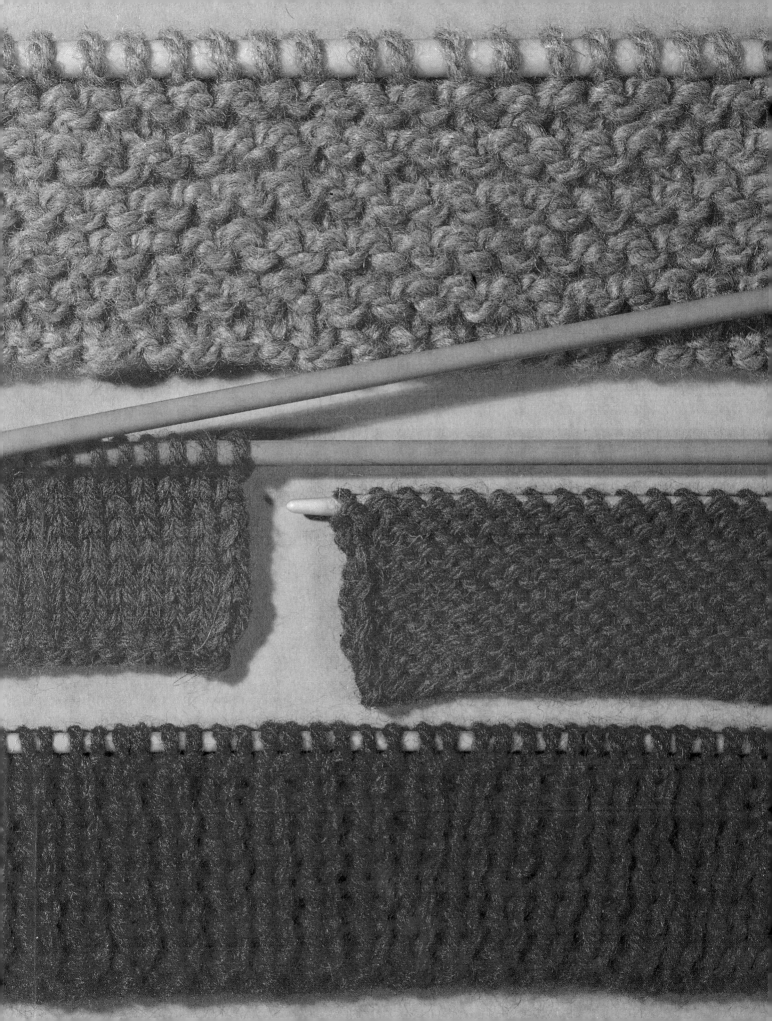

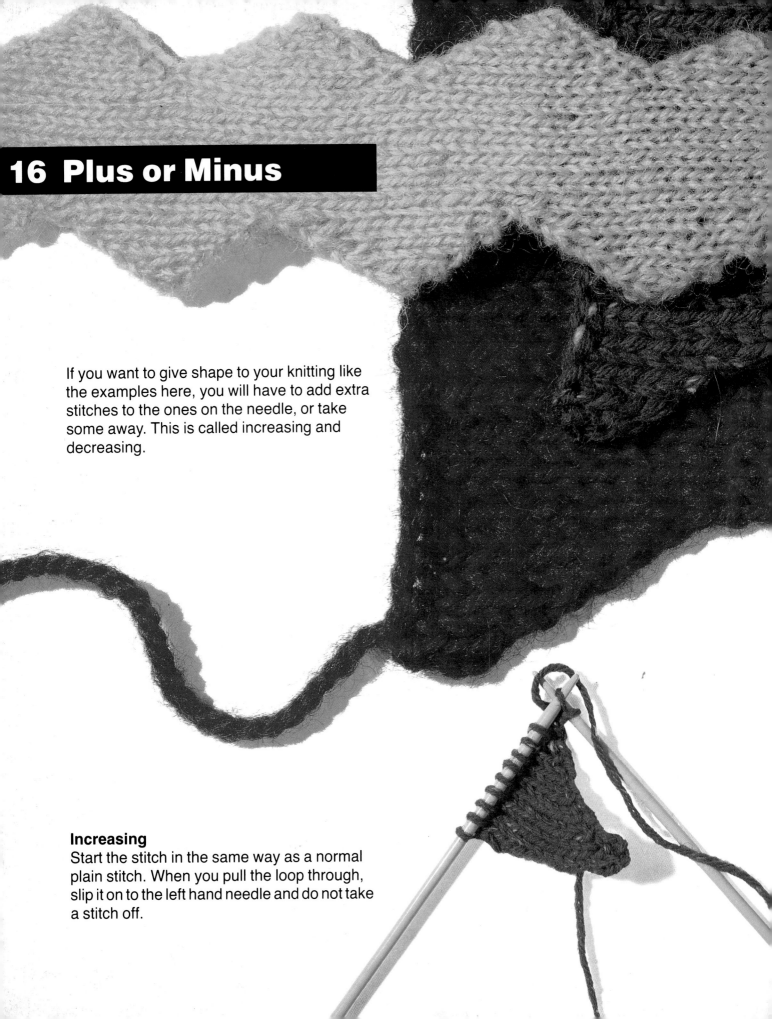

# 16 Plus or Minus

If you want to give shape to your knitting like the examples here, you will have to add extra stitches to the ones on the needle, or take some away. This is called increasing and decreasing.

**Increasing**
Start the stitch in the same way as a normal plain stitch. When you pull the loop through, slip it on to the left hand needle and do not take a stitch off.

## Decreasing

The simplest way to lose stitches is to knit two stitches together.

Increasing and decreasing can be used to give a decorative effect like the samples here, and also to shape armholes and necklines. If you follow a knitting pattern, it will tell you exactly how many stitches to increase or decrease.

# 18 Pompons

Try making pompons and tassels to decorate your garments. You could make them in the same colour as your garment, or in a contrasting colour.

## Tassels
Wrap a length of yarn round and round a small rectangle of card. Use a darning needle to slip a length of the same yarn under the top of the tassel and tie it in a knot. Use one end to wrap round the top of the tassel and the other end to attach the tassel to your knitting.

Try making multi-coloured tassels to decorate a scarf or the bottom of a jumper. You can use almost any type of yarn to make tassels.

## Pompons

Cut two circles of card to the size you want your pompon to be. Then cut holes in the middle of the circles. Place one circle on top of the other.

Wind some yarn into a small ball and wrap it round and round the card circles. When the hole in the middle has almost disappeared, cut the wool round the outside. Tie a length of yarn round the middle of the pompon between the two pieces of card. Remove the card circles.

Try making stripey pompons by winding different coloured yarns round the card circles. You could use your pompons to decorate a knitted hat!

# 20 Fringe & Plait

There are lots of different ways to make your knitting look exciting. One way is to add features, such as the fringing and plaits shown here.

## Fringing

Cut lengths of wool twice the length of the finished fringe. Bunch three or four strands together and fold them in two. Push a crochet hook through the edge of your knitting. Catch the loop of the fringe on the end of the crochet hook and pull it through to the other side. Poke the ends of the fringe through the loop and knot firmly. Continue in the same way at equal intervals. Fringing is often used to decorate the ends of scarves but it can also be used as a design feature on other garments.

## Plaiting

Bunch together some fairly long strands of yarn and tie them together with matching yarn at one end. Divide the strands into three equal sections. Fold the right hand section over the one to the left of it. Then fold the left hand section over the one to the right of it. Carry on until your plait is the length you want. Try making multi-coloured plaits, or use different textured yarns.

# 22 Appliqué

Here are some suggestions for decorating your knitting by adding buttons, bows, shells, ribbon and embroidery.

To make a ruffle like the one at the top, run a row of stitches along a narrow strip of knitting and pull the thread tight to gather the strip. You could make several ruffles and overlap them.

Stitch buttons and bows to your knitting with matching wool. You may need some help to pierce holes in shells so you can attach them. Look for other things, such as feathers, dry seed heads, flowers and old beads.

Large cross stitches made across your knitting will make a perfect slot to thread ribbon through.

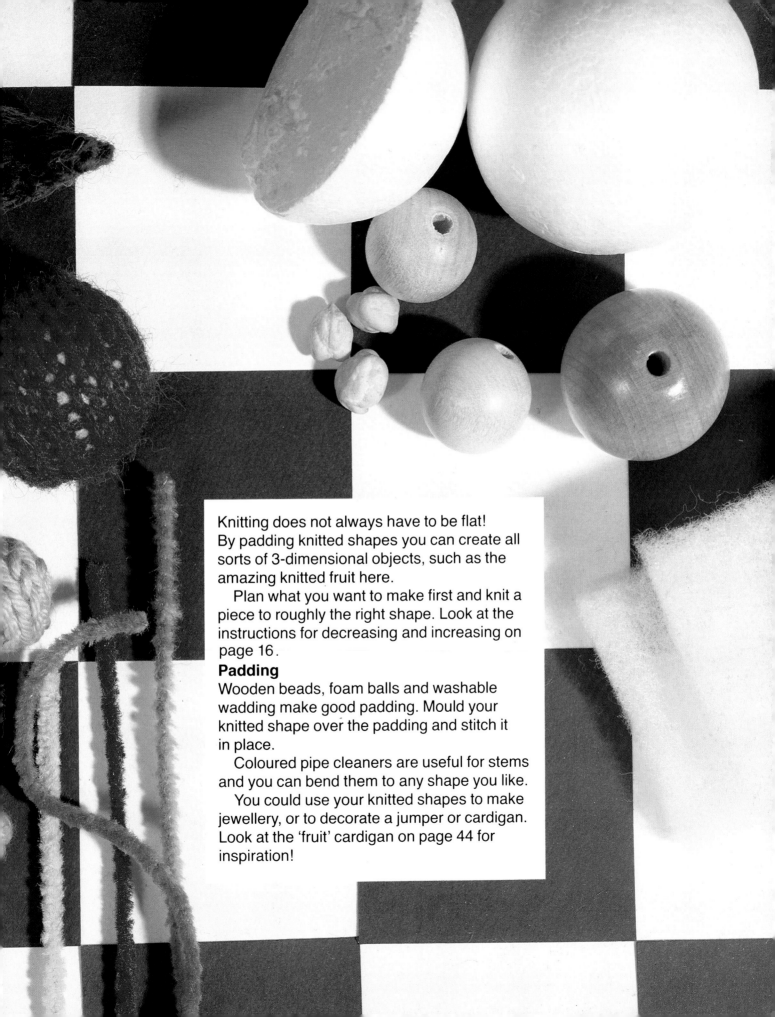

Knitting does not always have to be flat!
By padding knitted shapes you can create all
sorts of 3-dimensional objects, such as the
amazing knitted fruit here.

Plan what you want to make first and knit a
piece to roughly the right shape. Look at the
instructions for decreasing and increasing on
page 16.

**Padding**

Wooden beads, foam balls and washable
wadding make good padding. Mould your
knitted shape over the padding and stitch it
in place.

Coloured pipe cleaners are useful for stems
and you can bend them to any shape you like.

You could use your knitted shapes to make
jewellery, or to decorate a jumper or cardigan.
Look at the 'fruit' cardigan on page 44 for
inspiration!

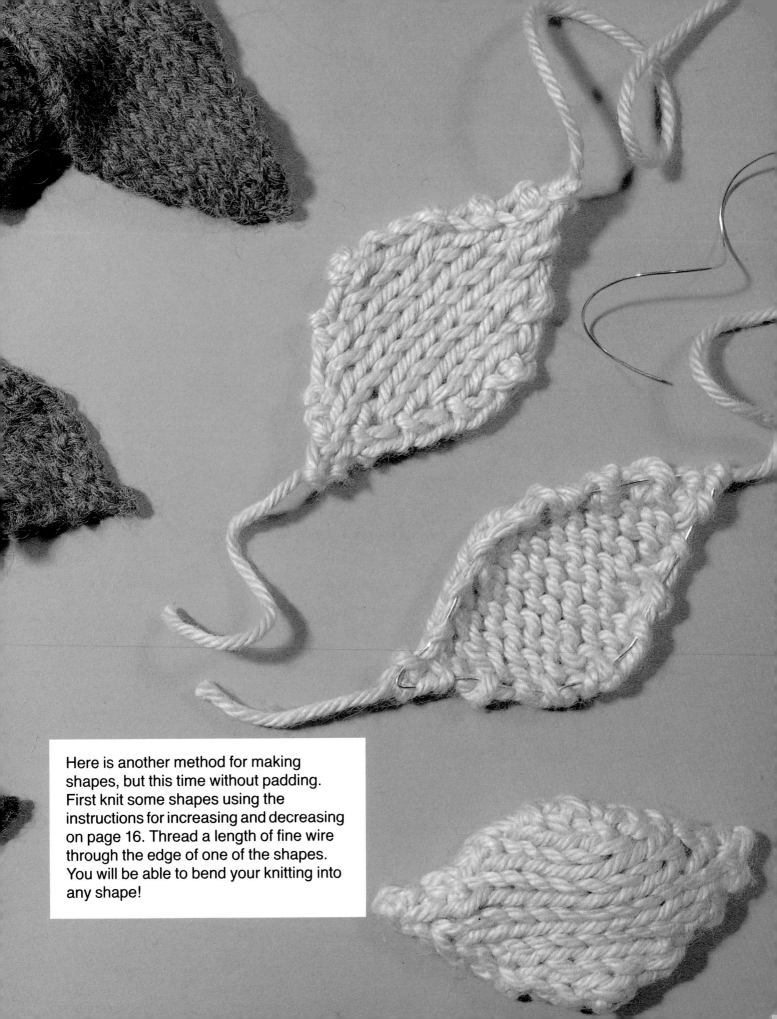

Here is another method for making shapes, but this time without padding. First knit some shapes using the instructions for increasing and decreasing on page 16. Thread a length of fine wire through the edge of one of the shapes. You will be able to bend your knitting into any shape!

# 28 Changing Colour

The simplest method for changing colour is to knit narrow stripes in contrasting colours. You can simply carry the yarn you are not using up the side of the garment until you need it again.

For wider stripes, break the yarn off when you have finished a colour and start again with the new colour. Knot the ends and weave them in on the wrong side.

If your design requires changing colours in the middle of a row and there are only a few stitches between the different colours you can carry the yarns loosely across the back of the work.

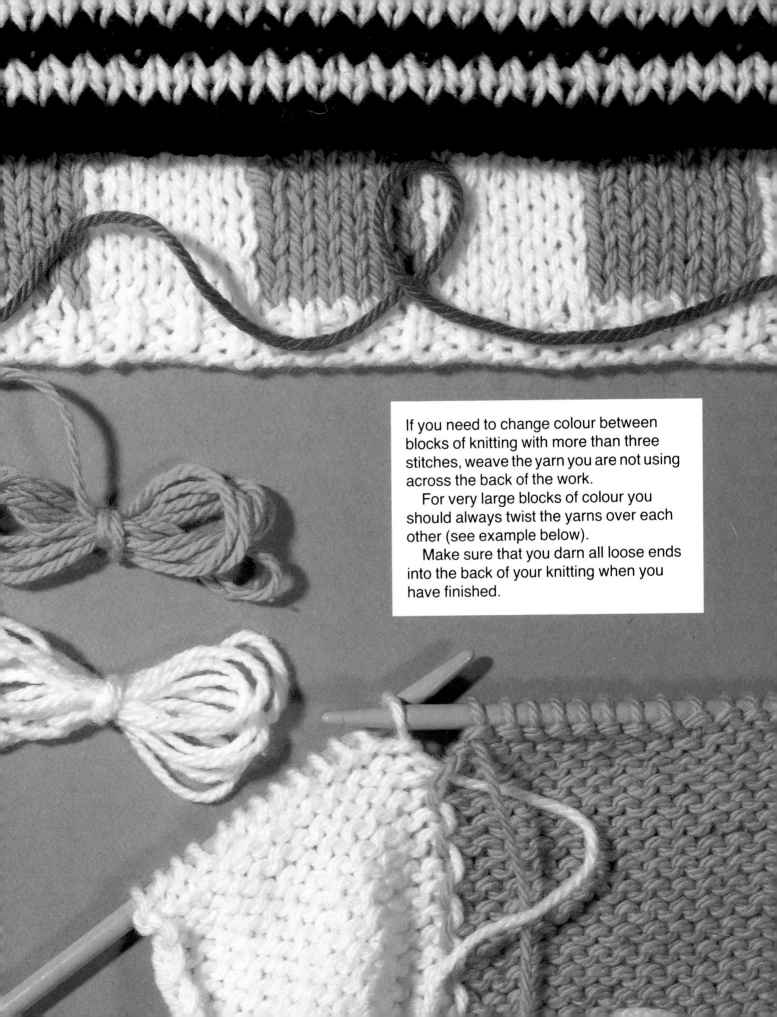

If you need to change colour between blocks of knitting with more than three stitches, weave the yarn you are not using across the back of the work.

For very large blocks of colour you should always twist the yarns over each other (see example below).

Make sure that you darn all loose ends into the back of your knitting when you have finished.

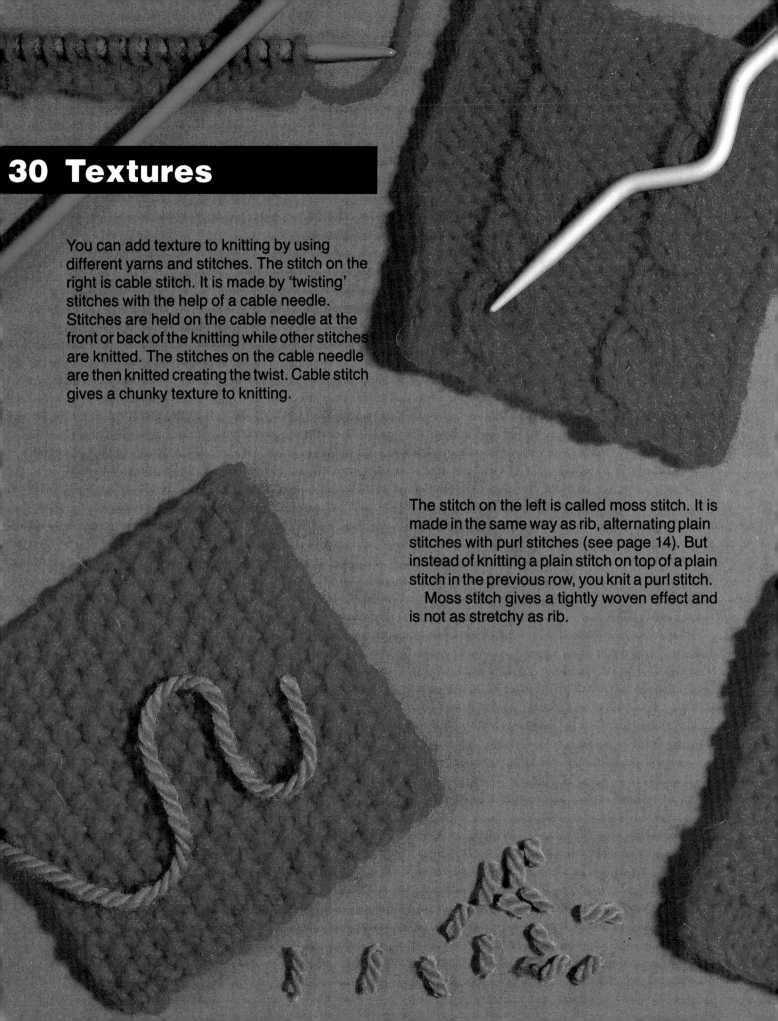

# 30 Textures

You can add texture to knitting by using different yarns and stitches. The stitch on the right is cable stitch. It is made by 'twisting' stitches with the help of a cable needle. Stitches are held on the cable needle at the front or back of the knitting while other stitches are knitted. The stitches on the cable needle are then knitted creating the twist. Cable stitch gives a chunky texture to knitting.

The stitch on the left is called moss stitch. It is made in the same way as rib, alternating plain stitches with purl stitches (see page 14). But instead of knitting a plain stitch on top of a plain stitch in the previous row, you knit a purl stitch.

Moss stitch gives a tightly woven effect and is not as stretchy as rib.

The stitch on the right is a lace stitch. There are lots of variations which you can find in books of knitting stitches — some are more complicated than others! Most lace stitches are based on increasing and decreasing stitches to make holes in the knitting. It is generally best to use a plain yarn so that the detail of the pattern shows up well.

The ridged sample on the left is very easy to knit. Knit a row of plain stitches followed by a row of purl stitches (see page 12). Knit eight rows of plain stitches. Continue knitting these ten rows in the same way.

Each time you experiment with a new stitch, keep a sample for future reference (see page 34).

# 32 Making Charts

Once you have had plenty of practice in knitting with one colour, you can experiment with creating pictures and patterns in several colours. To make a chart to work from, start with a simple design and draw or trace it on to squared paper. You can use pencils or felt-tip pens to indicate different colours, or you can make a key in the same way as we did with the sea horse. Each symbol represents a different colour.

When you start knitting your picture or pattern, remember that each square represents one stitch.

We used the sea and sea creatures for inspiration for our charts, but you may want to choose your own theme.

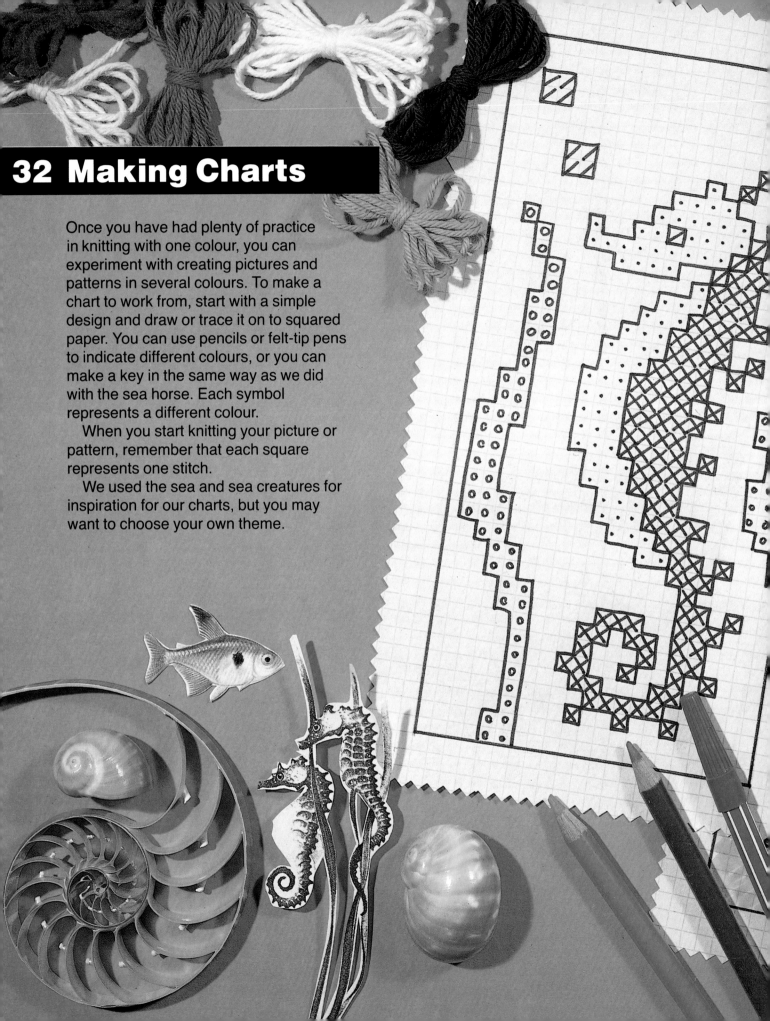

42

21

If you are attempting a complicated piece of knitting, it is best to knit a sample first. This will build your confidence for tackling a complete garment and will also give you the opportunity to experiment with different colours and yarns.

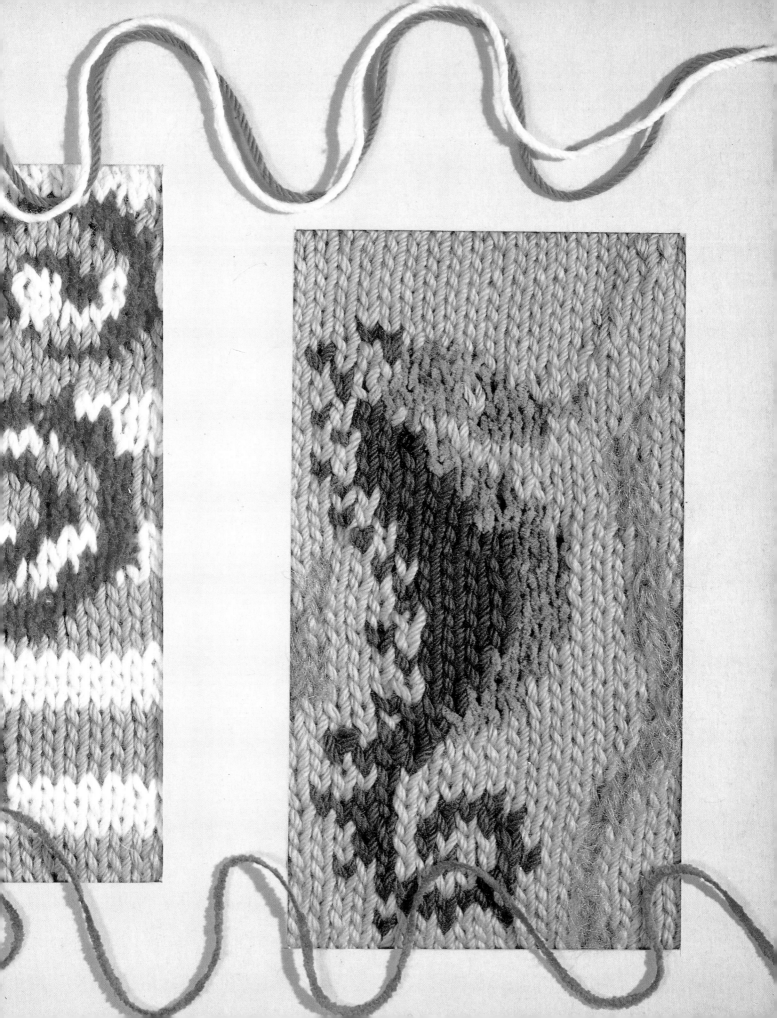

# 36 Design

When most people learn to knit they follow a pattern which has been created by a designer. But there is no reason why you cannot design your own garments.

Sketch out your ideas first, using squared paper to help you work out the proportions. Think about the type of yarn you want to use, colourways and stitches. You may want to include fringing, tassels, pompons or embroidery.

If you have built up a collection of yarns and swatches, these will be useful for inspiration!

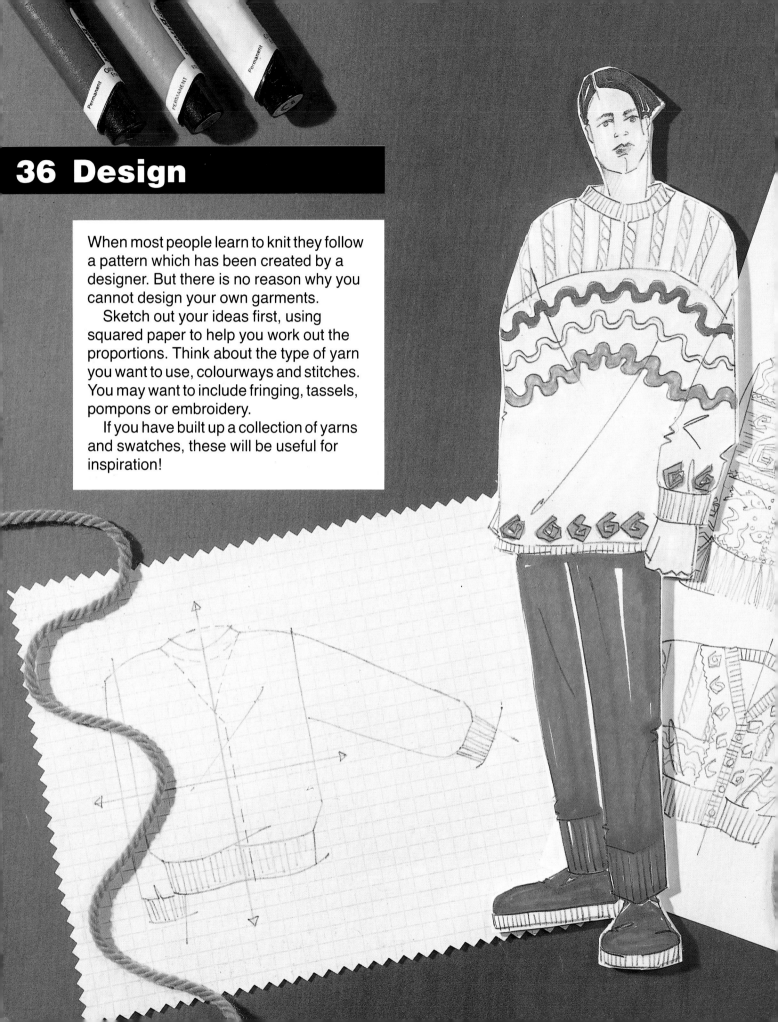

# 38 French Knitting

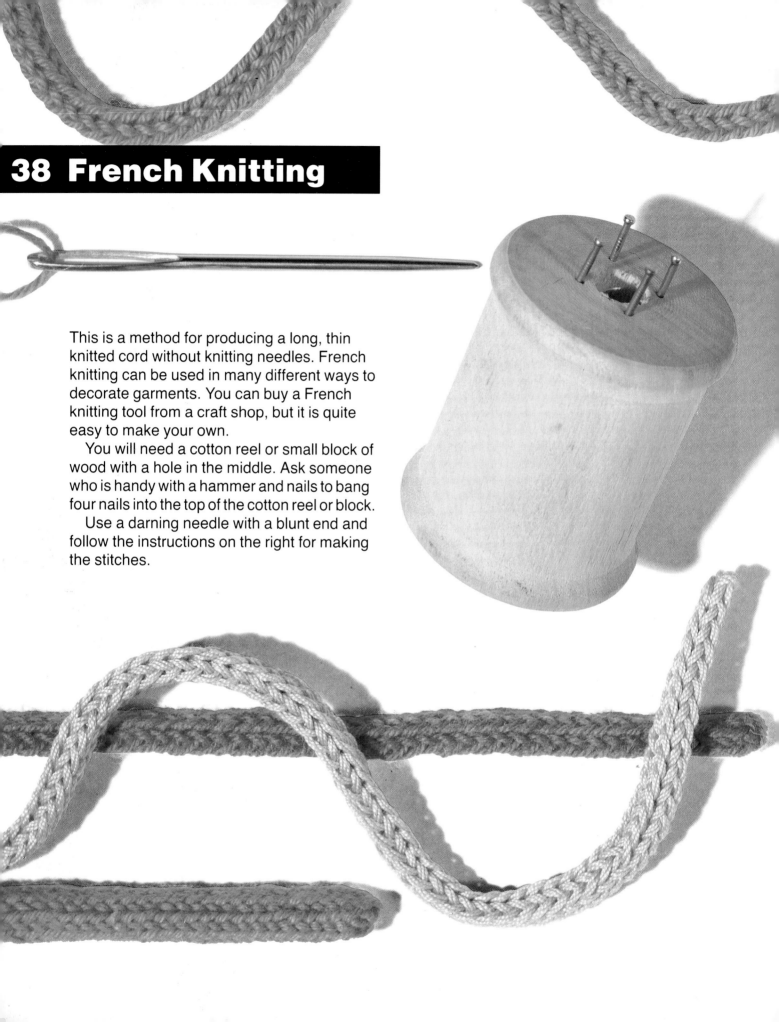

This is a method for producing a long, thin knitted cord without knitting needles. French knitting can be used in many different ways to decorate garments. You can buy a French knitting tool from a craft shop, but it is quite easy to make your own.

You will need a cotton reel or small block of wood with a hole in the middle. Ask someone who is handy with a hammer and nails to bang four nails into the top of the cotton reel or block.

Use a darning needle with a blunt end and follow the instructions on the right for making the stitches.

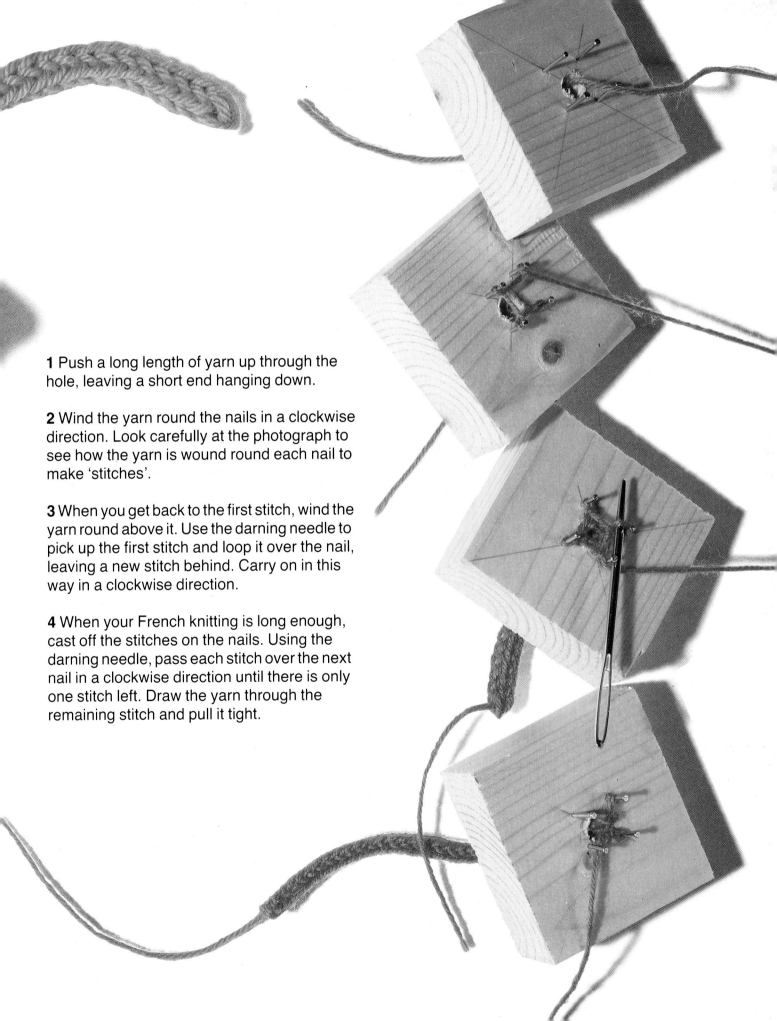

**1** Push a long length of yarn up through the hole, leaving a short end hanging down.

**2** Wind the yarn round the nails in a clockwise direction. Look carefully at the photograph to see how the yarn is wound round each nail to make 'stitches'.

**3** When you get back to the first stitch, wind the yarn round above it. Use the darning needle to pick up the first stitch and loop it over the nail, leaving a new stitch behind. Carry on in this way in a clockwise direction.

**4** When your French knitting is long enough, cast off the stitches on the nails. Using the darning needle, pass each stitch over the next nail in a clockwise direction until there is only one stitch left. Draw the yarn through the remaining stitch and pull it tight.

# 40 Hat & Scarf I

Try making a matching hat and scarf. You could choose the colours of your favourite football club, your school colours, or just your favourite colours!

# 42 Hat & Scarf II

## Scarves

Multi-coloured or plain, a long knitted scarf will keep you warm and cosy in the winter. Scarves can be thin or wide and knitted in any weight of yarn. If you use chunky yarn and thick needles, your knitting will grow more quickly. Finish the ends of your scarf off with a fringe (see page 20).

If you are knitting a stripey scarf, remember to break off the yarn each time you start a new colour. Darn the ends in afterwards.

## Hats
To knit a woolly hat like the one on the next page, cast on about 30 stitches. Knit approximately 8 cm of ribbing and then continue in stocking stitch. When the strip is long enough to fit over your head, knit another 8cm of ribbing and cast off. Sew up the sides of the hat and make a giant tassel for each corner. If you want the brim to turn over, knit 16 cm of ribbing at each end of the hat.

# 44 Adapting

Here are some suggestions for adapting and decorating your old sweaters to give them a new lease of life. We added knitted fruit to a cardigan and tassels to a stripey sweater. You could also experiment with adding coils of French knitting (see page 38).

# 46 Patterns

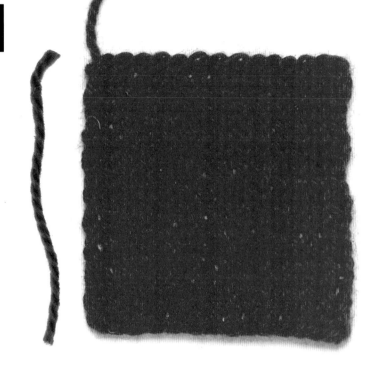

Knitting patterns may seem complicated at first, but when you get used to the abbreviations used you shouldn't have any trouble in following them. It is best to follow the pattern as you go, rather than reading it through first!

The pattern will tell you what type of yarn to use and how much you will need. It will also tell you what size needles to use. It is important to follow these instructions or the garment may end up too big or too small!

Most patterns suggest that you start by knitting a 'tension square'. This will show whether you are knitting too tightly or too loosely. You can adjust your tension by using thinner or thicker needles.

It is best to start with a fairly simple pattern without too much shaping or complicated stitches. If you choose a pattern which uses thick yarn and thick needles your knitting will grow quickly. You will need a tape measure, and a row counter which slips over the needle is also useful.

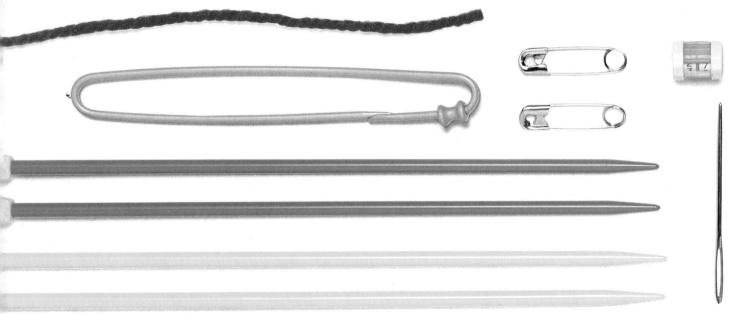

## Abbreviations

When you look at a knitting pattern you will find that most of the instructions are abbreviated to save space. Here are some of the abbreviations that are often used.

| | |
|---|---|
| **K** | knit |
| **P** | purl |
| **st** | stitch |
| **sts** | stitches |
| **inc** | increase |
| **dec** | decrease |
| **rep** | repeat |
| **beg** | begin |
| **foll** | following |
| **rem** | remaining |
| **st st** | stocking stitch |
| **alt** | alternate |
| **cont** | continue |
| **patt** | pattern |
| **mm** | millimetres |
| **cm** | centimetres |
| **RS** | right side |
| **WS** | wrong side |

# INDEX

Text and compilation copyright © Two-Can Publishing Ltd, 1991
Design copyright © Wendy Baker, 1991

This edition first published in Great Britain in 1991 by
Two-Can Publishing Ltd
in association with Scholastic Publications Ltd

Printed and bound in Hong Kong

2 4 6 8 10 9 7 5 3 1

British Library Cataloguing in Publication Data
Baker, Wendy
    Knitting – (Hands on)
    I. Title II. Series
    746.43

ISBN: 1–85434–100–6 (paperback)
ISBN: 1–85434–123–5 (hardback)

Photographs by Jon Barnes